NEW YORK DETAIL

A TREASURY OF ORNAMENTAL SPLENDOR

NEW YORK DETAIL

A TREASURY OF ORNAMENTAL SPLENDOR

Yumiko Kobayashi and Ryo Watanabe

CHRONICLE BOOKS

SAN FRANCISCO

First published in the United States in 1995 by Chronicle Books.

First published in Japan in 1993 by TOTO Publishing.

Text and photographs copyright© 1993 by Yumiko Kobayashi and Ryo Watanabe.

Printed in Singapore.

ISBN: 0-8118-1056-9

Library of Congress Cataloging in Publication Data available.

Cover design and composition: Carin Berger, Carin Berger Design

Distributed in Canada by

Raincoast Books

8680 Cambie Street

Vancouver, B.C. V6P 6M9

10 9 8 7 6 5 4 3 2 1

Chronicle Books

275 Fifth Street

San Francisco, California 94103

CONTENTS

It has been just over five years since Ryo Watanabe and I returned to Tokyo – the city where we were born and grew up – and began again our life here. Nevertheless, we still miss some things about New York: the stimulating friendships, the operas and concerts (they are so expensive in Tokyo that we can't just go whenever the mood strikes us), the exhibitions at museums and galleries, the flea markets, the sounds, the air, the ambiance – and, above all, the city itself.

While we were in New York, we often enjoyed just wandering around: leaving our loft on Hester Street on the Lower East Side, eating dim sum in nearby Chinatown, walking through Little Italy, going to SoHo to drop by a gallery, then paying a visit to Greenwich Village, or just going straight up Bowery to the East Village galleries to check out the work being done by young artists. Sometimes we sat near the Fulton Fish Market or the deck of Pier 17 and passed the time watching boats plying the East River, or walked across the Brooklyn Bridge to see Manhattan from the other side, or we took the bus or subway to visit the museums in Central Park or in uptown or midtown Manhattan.

Of course, Tokyo is not completely lacking in such entertainments. Some say that Tokyo is interesting because of its so-called "street style," like that of the city shown in the movie *Blade Runner*, but Tokyo really is just a gigantic village, one that expanded without adequate urban planning. Its classic buildings, mainly of wood, are difficult to preserve and are being lost because the city has no effective preservation policy. The places Ryo and I love are scattered here and there around the town, isolated in the midst of new construction. And so we have become deprived of the joy of wandering.

Living in New York City, we were surprised to find so much urban history, especially considering America's youthfulness. Before taking up residence there, it was our understanding that the buildings we should see in New York – and the United States – were modern and contemporary architecture, and that prior to Art Deco, Louis Sullivan, and Frank Lloyd Wright, the only architectural style was that of "stylism," a mere pasting together of old European styles. But once we began to live in New York and to wander its streets, we came to realize that much of the charm of this city is based on the prevalence of its premodern architecture, including many unsung buildings. Great slabs of material, a grid pattern of streets, and even huge masses of overwhelming height provided an orderly setting without coldly shutting us out or condescending to us or boring us. As we surveyed the streets from a distance, the buildings seemed only a part of the overall texture, but once we drew closer we saw that they were richly expressive due to the wide variety of ornaments. This was our first encounter with the entities called ornaments. We decided that it was due to rapidly changing fads in architectural direction and the patchwork of various styles – both characteristic of New York's premodern architecture – that such a rich variety of ornaments are concentrated in this limited area of the island of Manhattan.

When we walk through the streets of the business areas of midtown Manhattan, where modern and contemporary architectural structures stand side by side, many buildings nearly a century old stand out. In Manhattan as a whole, the number of buildings done in the combination of styles that predated modern architecture is remarkably large. The decorative Art Nouveau movement, a reaction to traditional nineteenth-century design styles, was popular in the United States from the end of the nineteenth century through the thirties, when these buildings were built (and in Europe from the 1890s to the 1910s). This was also a time of revolutionary change in architecture, which was moving toward the total negation of ornamentation, as found in the work of Adolf Loos (1870-1939) and in the International style of the 1920s.

In the American architectural world, the avant-garde Chicago School began constructing steel-frame skyscrapers in the 1880s. In contrast, the East Coast, including New York City, was dominated by the conservative style of architects McKim, Mead & White, among others. Ironically, the World's Columbian Exposition, held in Chicago in 1893, ended up as only a Chicago School avant-garde experiment, and so this grand show helped to cause a reversion to stylism. As a result, New York architecture continued to use classical elements until modernization was ushered in by Art Deco in the 1930s.

Old buildings decorated with ornaments are spread throughout Manhattan. In the Upper East Side, Yorkville, Chelsea, and the Upper West Side, many small townhouses are still in good condition because their construction was rather late. Even in midtown Manhattan, which is now under invasion by contemporary architecture, there are Art Deco office and commercial buildings and Gothic Revival churches. The area around Greenwich Village was developed in the 1820s, and the Federal style of that era remains. SoHo is filled with cast-iron buildings. A lot of low-income apartment buildings, once called tenement houses, still stand in the Lower East Side, though they are in various states of decay and disrepair. Wall Street and the area to the south, which were developed earliest, still contain many skyscraper office buildings with terra-cotta facades and buildings which are like monuments to early development. In New York City, the style of the buildings varies depending on when they were built and the purposes they were built to fulfill.

TINPLATE PEDIMENTS

Manhattan's oldest existing building is said to be St. Paul's Chapel of Trinity Parish (Broadway and Fulton Street), built in 1766. This church survived a fire in 1778 that burned a thousand structures, or about a quarter of the city at that time. The church also escaped annihilation in a 1783 fire that reduced some three thousand structures to ashes. Some architectural historians call buildings from the 1790s to the 1830s Modified Georgian, but they are now commonly called Federal style because they were built following the Revolutionary War. The style is completely nonornamental, with long rectangular windows set into brick walls. A few other buildings from around this time can still be found in Greenwich Village.

Most of the older buildings in New York that were constructed after the American Civil War (1861-65) were low-income apartment buildings, then known as tenement houses. In 1900, there were 42,700 tenement houses in Manhattan due to a sharp increase in the city's population, including a surge in immigration. Gorgeous apartment buildings like the Dakota (1 West 72nd Street), built in 1884, were exceptions. Tenement houses were built as cheaply as possible. In order to hide the lack of such amenities as service facilities, natural lighting, and proper ventilation, landlords competed with each other to construct the most attractive ornamental facades. A typical tenement house stood five to six stories high on a twenty-five-by-one-hundred-foot lot, was of brick construction, and faced the street with four long, mass-produced, wood-frame, double-hung windows per story. Entranceways, window surrounds, and cornices were ornamented as elegantly as possible. The decorations for such apartments were made of metal, thanks to the development of the steel industry and mass production during the Industrial Revolution. Cornices, keystones, and other elements were expensive when made of stone or wood, but molded galvanized steel (tinplate) cornices and pediments, terra-cotta, and molded mortar keystones were much more reasonable in price. By combining different ready-made parts, a unique facade could be constructed for landlords desiring high return for a minimal investment. Many of the cornices and pediments shown in this book belong to such tenement houses and show the wide variety of combinations that were employed.

As a result of regulations aimed at improving living conditions, tenement houses were later upgraded in regard to their amenities, access to natural light, and ventilation. But the outside appearance of many of these buildings remained the same except for fire escapes, which were installed outside the windows. One such structure is the seven-story walk-up loft building on the east side of SoHo, where we lived. Originally it was not an apartment building but a sewing factory, commonly called a "sweat shop," and the staircase spirals around a central hoist (a rope pulley with a manually operated loader). Each floor has pipes that had been used for gaslights protruding from the walls. A typical structure of its kind, there are no partitions except for bathrooms and closets on each of the floors, which are generally twenty-five by seventy-five feet. The brick walls (two feet thick on the first and second floors, one foot thick on the other floors) have oak beams with a one-foot pitch, and the floor is of thick oak. Molded tinplate ceilings were used for fire protection and emergency steel fire escapes hang outside the front and rear of the building. All of these elements have deteriorated over the nearly one hundred years since the building was built. In our loft, fugitive light beams pierced through cracks in the floor, and one day a strong wind blew a loose pane of glass out of its sash. Every year before the onset of winter, all eighteen windows had to be covered with vinyl sheets. The brick structure of the outside walls is as damaged as the other parts of the building: Weathering has reduced the mortar between the bricks to a sandlike powder. But the thick walls have good thermal properties, and these bricks and their oak beams and floors, which have supported the nearly ten-foot-high ceilings for so many years, boast an attractiveness that cannot be denied and create a comfortable living space.

ORNAMENTATION STARTED WITH THE JOINTS

Around the turn of the century, the typical building materials in New York City were cast iron and terra-cotta. Cast-iron architecture used a construction technique called post and lintel: Mass-produced cast-iron pillars and beams were selected and matched from a catalog, then were bolted together at the construction site. This was a completely different technique from that used in conventional masonry structures. First used in the 1840s, it made possible expansive facades with large openings and spacious interiors that were not possible in masonry structures. This technique was frequently used in warehouses and other buildings, especially in SoHo and Tribeca. Cast-iron architecture pointed to the direction that steel-construction architecture would take, but the low-precision cast-iron beams had strength limitations and were replaced with steel beams, which allowed the construction of taller buildings. The first building in New York to use steel beams was the Cooper Union building, which was completed in 1859. In this building, however, the steel beams simply abutted an exterior brownstone wall as replacements for the traditional wooden beams. It was 1889 – four years after the first steel-frame skyscraper was built in Chicago – before New York saw independent steel-construction architecture such as we are familiar with today.

Steel-construction architecture was developed based on the technical demands of skyscrapers. Most of the designs used in these buildings, however, were based on those of masonry structures. Terra-cotta became very popular because a material lighter than stone was needed to compensate for the increasing height of the buildings, as well as for the fact that steel construction was neither fireproof nor weatherproof.

In addition to the familiar deep red-brown, terra-cotta came in a variety of different colors such as an ivory unglazed bisque that looked like limestone, and the brightly glazed hues seen in Art Deco buildings. The shapes were not limited just to those of mass-produced terra-cotta; much original, high-quality work was done by sculptors, which added personality and variety to entire buildings.

The more we look at these ornaments, the more we realize that they were not used simply for decoration. Take labels, for instance. Labels are slightly projecting areas forming part of the masonry arch near entrances and windows, which act to shunt raindrops running down the wall over to the side. The ends of these labels are carefully terminated with bosses, called label stops. Small projecting parts such as openings for entrances and windows, which are easy to make in today's reinforced concrete structures, in masonry structures require the support of corbels and brackets, as well as crossing arches and lintels. Thus were ornaments born from the practical requirements of specific construction materials and techniques.

The design of building details is important because the details determine the overall appearance of a building. It is particularly difficult to design those areas where elements meet one another. As architect Louis I. Kahn (1901-74) said, "The joint is the beginning of ornament." (*What Will Be Has Always Been: The Words of Louis I. Kahn* by Richard Saul Wurman).

Keystones that have been removed from their buildings and placed in a museum garden or sold by antiques dealers look like empty shells, removed as they are from their positions as wedges within arches. Partially burned-out buildings, their ornaments ripped off like knocked-out teeth, alone on some deserted slum area street; brownstone carvings and keystone faces that suddenly fall off one day because of the winds and rains of many years – these are the fates of buildings that are not protected as landmarks by the New York City Landmark Preservation Commission. Our hope is that the beautiful and diverse ornaments in this book, the heritage of a changing city, will quietly survive forever.

INTRODUCTION

Architectural ornaments are mysterious entities that we usually notice only peripherally if at all because they are subsumed within a building's overall appearance, even though they exist right on its surface. In fact, some New Yorkers may have never seen the interesting ornaments across the street from where they have lived for many years. It was only after we began taking pictures that we realized how many ornaments exist in Manhattan, even though we had remarked on them before. When we began to walk around with our camera, tripod, map, pen, and notebook, without any previous knowledge of ornaments or their styles, we made it our rule to shoot only what we thought interesting. When the quantity of our developed Kodachromes reached a certain level, we started to put them in some kind of order. It was only after doing this that we began to collect and survey books on art history and ornamentation.

We thought of several ways to sort the data: by architectural styles, which, characteristic of New York architecture until the 1930s, went through many quick changes – Greek Revival, Gothic Revival, Italian Traditional, Victorian Gothic, and a wildly commingled style called Gilded Age Kitchen Sink; by structural components; and by materials. We eventually decided on the categories of structural components and materials because we were interested in ornaments as architectural detail rather than as superficial stylistic elements. Also, we wanted to create a book in which an entire building could be seen through its structural components, and entire streets could be seen by looking at their buildings. We added the sections on cast iron, terra-cotta, and metalwork because we wanted to summarize New York design around the turn of the century using another important element in the determination of architectural design: materials. Consequently, the categories tend to overlap.

The first summer we began our project we went out shooting nearly every day unless it rained. It was a job that strained our necks more than our feet as we walked around viewing buildings from top to bottom and on both sides of the street while checking them off on our map. We made it a rule to take our shots from street level. It was the only way to take as many photographs as possible, but it is also true that these ornaments were created to be seen from the street. Sculptures, for example, were created with enlarged faces so that they would appear natural when seen from below. At first, neither of us expected we would become so involved in the picture-taking process. These ornaments, after all, were just simple decorations, a kind of taboo to us, who had been educated in the "less is more" doctrine of modernism. Furthermore, most of New York's ornaments were just reiterations of past styles. Nevertheless, once we began to take our photographs, we were amazed by the high quality, the diversity of styles, and the rich variety of these architectural elements.

Each morning we ventured forth with a general idea of what we wanted to photograph. From our loft on the east side of SoHo, we took a bus or subway if our destination was far away, or if it was nearby, we walked, then studiously zigzagged around. We often needed to reshoot because of varying light conditions. It was not always pleasant taking pictures, as we sometimes had to deal with people who were wandering the early-morning streets lost on heroin, or with homeless people who yelled at us for no discernible reason, but a lot of interesting ornaments are found in questionable areas. There were buildings half burned down by accidental fires set by drug addicts who had sneaked into the empty buildings to start fires for melting heroin or for sterilizing their needles. There were buildings from which the ornaments had been stolen because of an increase in their commercial value. It seemed that many buildings with fine ornaments were fated to disappear in the not-too-distant future, except for those designated as landmarks.

TERRA-COTTA

Terra-cotta became popular as an alternative to brownstone, a material that was easy to produce but that could not stand up to freezing temperatures. Moreover, a material lighter than stone was required due to the increasing height of buildings. Whether unglazed or glazed bright red, yellow, blue, green, or glossy white, it is weatherproof and strong; it can be finely delineated, yet be mass produced easily; and it can echo original design. With the spread of steel construction and the development of the skyscraper, terra-cotta was also popular because it was fireproof, which steel-constructed buildings were not. Until the American terra-cotta industry was developed in the 1870s, most of this material was imported from England.

CAST IRON

One of the major characteristics of New York architecture around the turn of the century is the growth of iron and steel construction, made possible by the development and mass production of metal products during the Industrial Revolution. Cast iron, which was used extensively in warehouses and factories in SoHo, allowed the use of large openings and large interior spaces, which were impossible with masonry structures. Cast iron also made new design elements possible, such as large glass show windows for midtown commercial buildings. In the 1840s, a prefabrication method called post and lintel allowed architects to select cast-iron parts from catalogs and to freely combine them. Pillars and beams manu-

factured at factories were bolted together on site. Cast iron could not match the strength of steel, however, and steel construction replaced cast iron as the height and length of spans were increased.

METALWORK

Much of the elaborate designs of the Art Deco period were expressed in metalwork. The variety of metal ornaments includes sheet-metal ornaments with raised reliefs; molded ornaments using cast-iron techniques; and simple and cheap ornaments made by cutting or bending metal.

KEYSTONE

A wedge-shaped stone that sits at the center of an arch. Human faces are often used as a motif, but angels, animals, plants, abstract patterns, and gargoyles also appear. Of interest are Native American faces, unique to America, and the fish motifs that can be found near the Fulton Fish Market. Keystones were mostly made of brownstone, limestone, and terra-cotta, though severe weathering has partly obliterated many of the brownstone keystones. Some later keystones were merely decorative shapes formed of cast iron and other materials.

CORBEL, BRACKET, AND LABEL STOP

Corbel: A block jutting from the wall to support loads like cornices, arches, bay windows, and pilasters at the top of masonry structures. Some are step shaped. Many can be seen in Romanesque, Gothic, and other architectural styles.

Bracket: An overhanging member that supports elements that protrude from a wall, such as

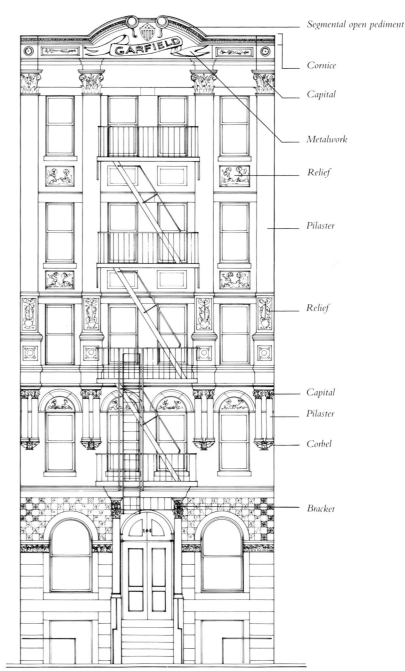

Segmental open pediment

Cornice

Capital

Metalwork

Relief

Pilaster

Relief

Capital

Pilaster

Corbel

Bracket

104 FORSYTH STREET

An example of a tenement house. The name on the pediment, molded from sheet iron, is Garfield, probably referring to the president who took office in 1881 only to be assassinated later that same year. The architect and completion date are unknown.

balconies, pediments, cornices, and the like. A variety of materials were used, including stone, wood, metal, and terra-cotta.
Label stop: Drip moldings at entranceways and windows are called labels, or drip molds; their terminating decorations are called label stops and were executed in motifs such as human faces. The materials are mainly stone and terra cotta.

ANCHOR

Masonry-structure architecture is constructed using wooden beams and brick or stone masonry, but sometimes facing walls are reinforced with steel or iron belts to prevent the walls from bulging outward. An anchor is a metal fixture that terminates the rod protruding from the exterior wall. A beam anchor fastens a wooden beam and its support to a masonry-structure wall. Many are star-shaped or dart-shaped; others are shaped like flowers, numbers, lion faces, or starfish – all entertaining to our eyes.

HERM AND TERMINUS

In ancient Greece, a pillar topped with the head of the god Hermes was used as a milestone; thus the origin of the name of this ornament. A herm is an armless bust of a man or woman, placed atop a square pillar that tapers toward the bottom. A terminus is a statuelike torso that protrudes from a console, bracket, or other such element. Often they are symmetrically positioned on both sides of entranceways, as if standing guard. The materials used are primarily stone and terra-cotta.

CAPITAL

The head of a column or pilaster. There are a number of variations, from Grecian Ionic, Doric, and Corinthian styles to styles that vary according to time and place. The materials are mainly stone and terra-cotta. One characteristic of New York capitals is that a number of them are made of cast iron. Some of their Corinthian-style acanthus leaf decorations were individually molded.

WALLS

Brownstone, which for some time was the basic building material for townhouses, could not withstand severe winter freezes, so it was eventually replaced with terra-cotta, limestone, and other materials. The exterior walls of the buildings around the turn of the century in New York are mostly made of brick, terra-cotta, and limestone, and on rare occasions "cast stone"(molded mortar). Many walls are similar in their colors and textures. Glazed terra-cotta is conspicuous in its bright coloration. Reliefs and carvings of stone, terra-cotta, and other materials are often seen as wall-surface ornaments decorating the spaces above and below windows, and the panels to the left and right of the arches, called spandrels.

OPENINGS

Windows, entrances, and other openings are important elements in defining the overall impression of a facade. Because of the structural limitations of masonry, most windows are vertically longer and double-hung. In a typical tenement house, four such windows line up per floor, and lintels cross above the windows. Decorative

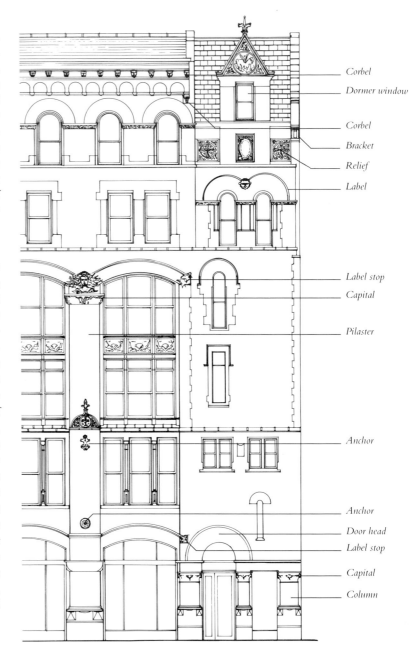

Corbel

Dormer window

Corbel

Bracket

Relief

Label

Label stop

Capital

Pilaster

Anchor

Anchor

Door head

Label stop

Capital

Column

376–380 LAFAYETTE STREET
Henry J. Harderbergh, Architect, 1888
By the architect who designed the Dakota apartments and the Plaza Hotel.
An example of Romanesque Revival.

lintels – arch, with keystones or surmounted with pediments – can be seen. On rare occasions early apartment houses had overhanging windows, called bay windows or, if in the attic, dormer windows. Labels were placed around prominent areas such as entranceways and their surrounds to provide shelter from the rain. Many labels are decorated with arches and pediments, or are porch shaped and supported by corbels, brackets, or other elements.

ROOFS

Most roofs of the buildings in this book are classic revivals that use cornices, pediments, and so forth. Variations were created by combining parts. Pediments sometimes have the name of a president of the era or the name of the original owner's wife. Many are inscribed with the year the building was built. Numerous tenement houses are still standing today, but their sheet-iron parts are severely damaged from exposure to wind and rain over the years. Standard pediments include triangular gables. Pediments with broken tops are known as broken pediments. Other shapes include scrolled pediments, with curving sea shapes or foliage patterns, and segmental pediments shaped like a bow. Terra-cotta and stone pediments, parapets, gables, and other roof elements are rare.

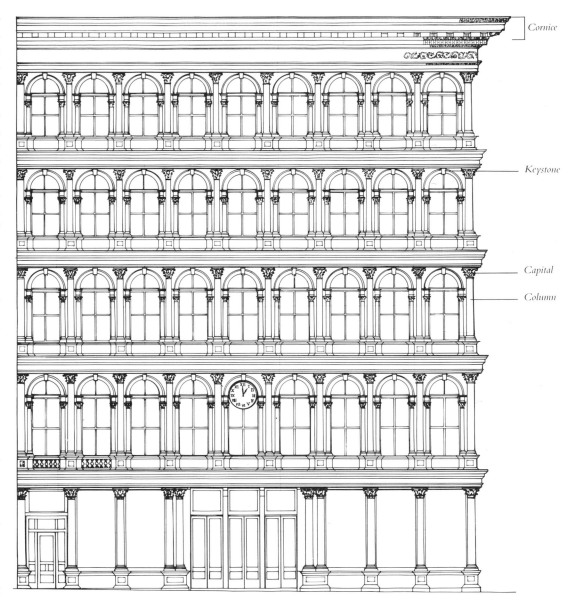

Cornice

Keystone

Capital

Column

HAUGHWOUT BUILDING

488-492 Broadway, John P. Gaynor, Architect, 1857

A typical example of post-and-lintel cast-iron construction.

MATERIALS

CAST IRON

Cast iron allowed the use of wide openings and wide interior spaces that were impossible with masonry structures and made such new features as large show windows feasible.

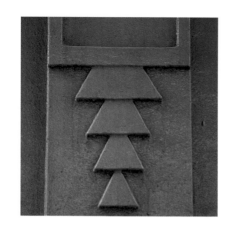

Whether unglazed or glazed in bright colors, terra-cotta is weatherproof and strong. Because it can be finely shaped and easily mass produced, it was often used for original design work in place of brownstone.

  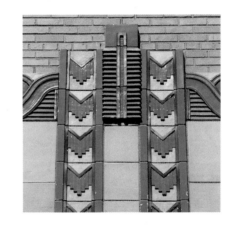

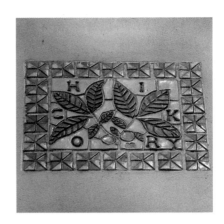

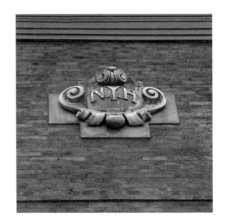

METALWORK

Some metalwork is sheet metal with a raised relief, while other kinds are molded or made from cut and shaped pieces. Metalwork was often used to express the streamlined motifs of the Art Deco era.

DETAILS

KEYSTONES

Most keystones are brownstone, limestone, or terra-cotta, but the majority of brownstone keystones have been severely damaged by weather. The major motif is the human face; other motifs include animals, plants, and fish.

CORBELS, BRACKETS, AND LABEL STOPS

A variety of decorations can be seen in the brackets that support elements projecting from exterior walls.

The materials used include stone, wood, metal, and terra-cotta.

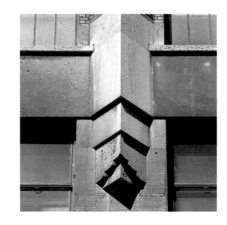

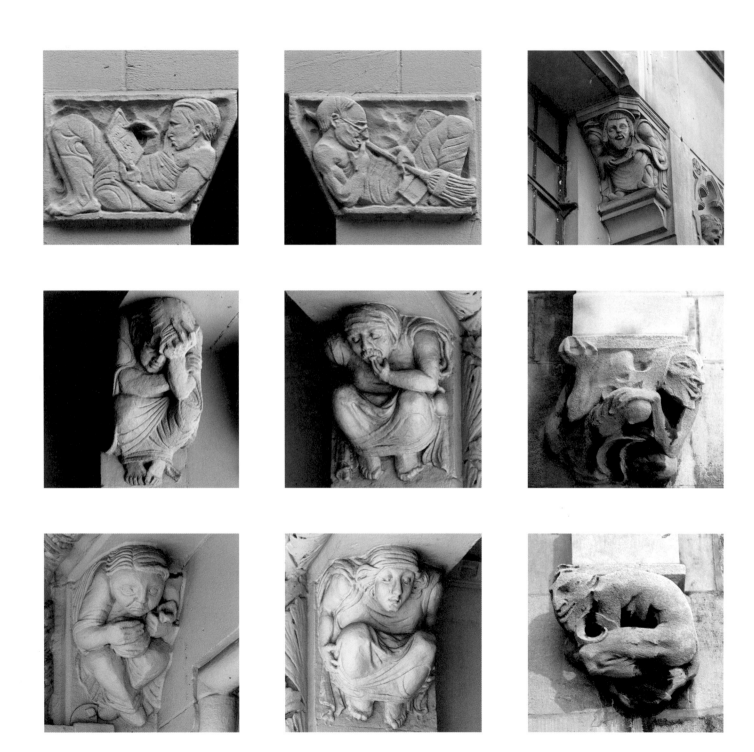

HERMS AND TERMINUSES

Armless busts of men and women and statues of human torsos are often positioned symmetrically on both sides of entrance areas like guardians of the gate.

CAPITALS

The heads of columns and pilasters have many variations, from Greek styles to those that run the gamut of periods and places. Elsewhere mainly made of stone and terra-cotta, cast-iron capitals are characteristic of New York.

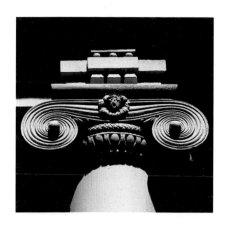  

 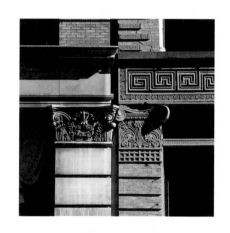 

65 | *capitals*

ANCHORS

Anchors terminate reinforcing steel rods that prevent stone or brick walls from bulging outward. Many are shaped like stars or darts; others are found in such delightful shapes as flowers, numbers, and lion faces.

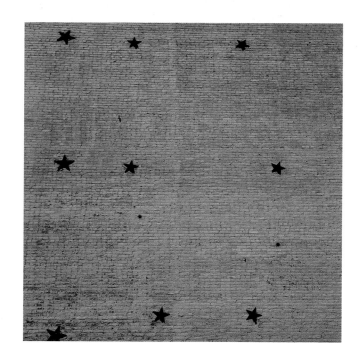

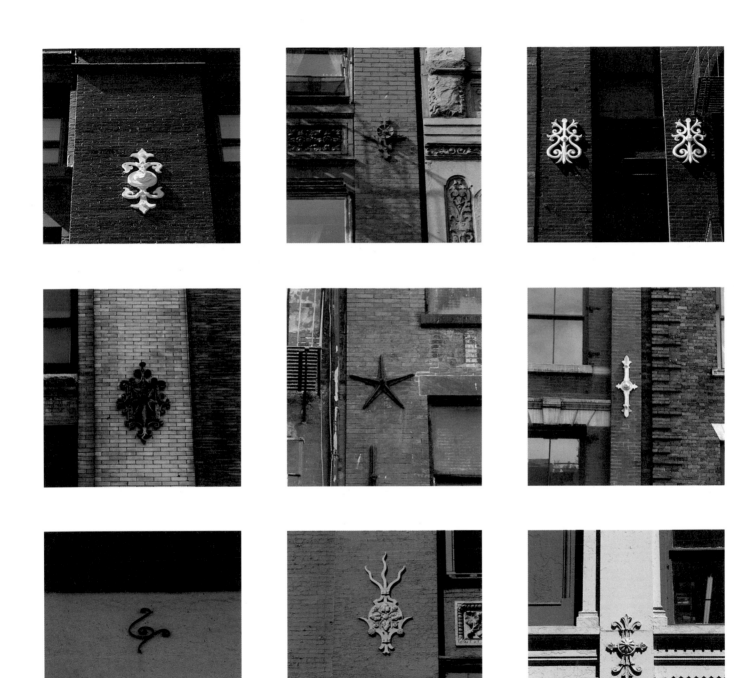

FACADES

WALLS

The exterior walls of this period were made of brick, terra-cotta, or limestone. Many are similar in both color and texture. Glazed terra-cotta ornaments are conspicuous in their bright coloration.

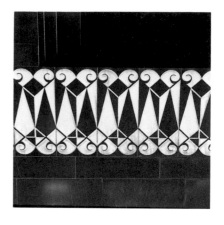

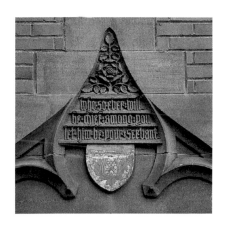

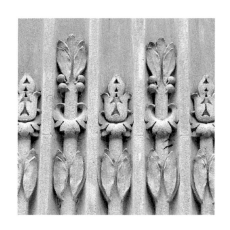

OPENINGS

Decorative openings include arches with keystones and crossing lintels above some windows, as well as pediments.

Labels are sometimes placed around entrances, the most conspicuous part of the facade. Some entrances are

shaped like porches and are supported by corbels and brackets with arches or pediments.

ROOFS

Overwhelmingly done in a classic revival style using cornices and pediments, roofs show great variety in their combinations of elements. Pediments may be inscribed with the year of construction, or the name of the current president, or the original owner's wife.

ANNA ESPOSITO 1926

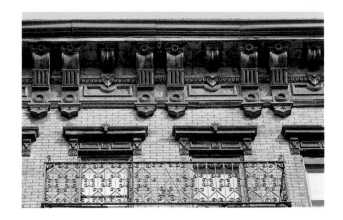

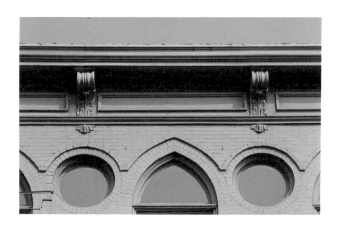 

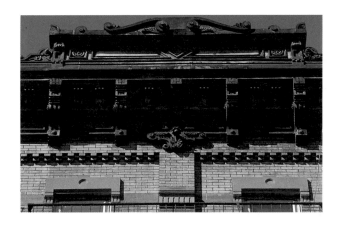

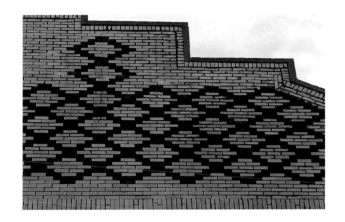

MANHATTAN

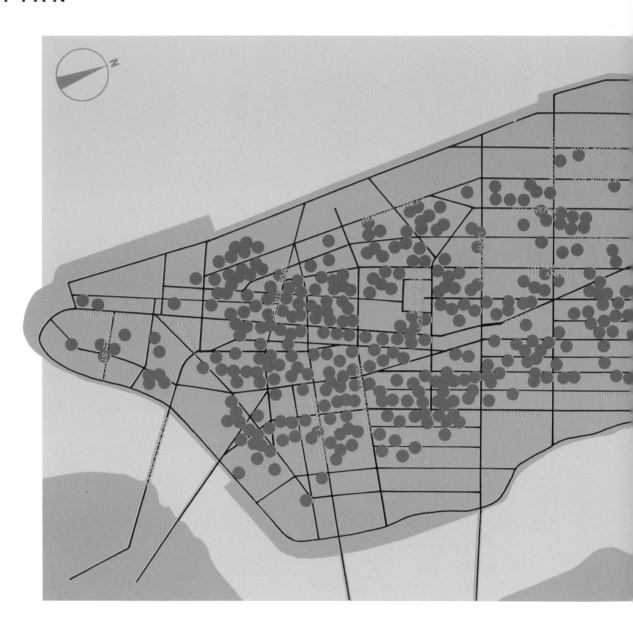

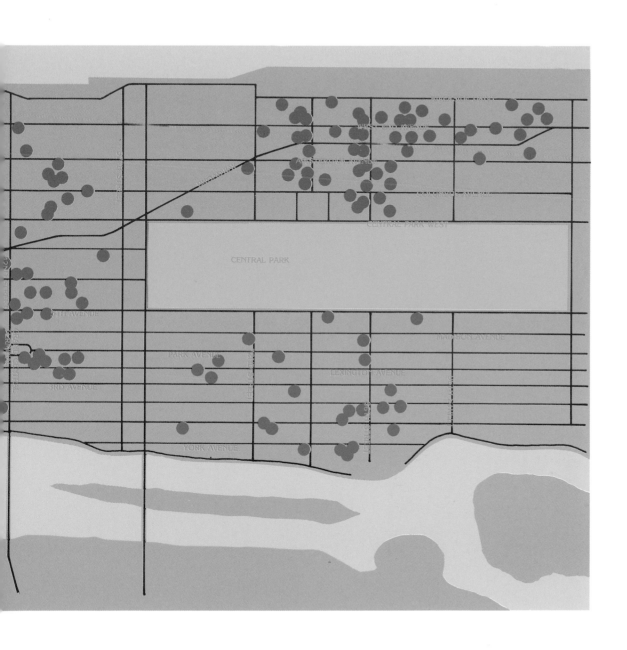

AFTERWORD

Cross-pollination makes everyone richer. The architectural ornaments of Italy are elegant and beautiful, but they do not have the variety and freshness of the ornaments of New York, which are the result of the combination of many different architectural heritages. If you stand at the top of the grand staircase of Grand Central Station and look down, you will be amazed by the multicolored waves of so many different kinds of hair. In New York, people of every color of skin and type of language, from all levels of society, live together. Because of this, New York is a city of both dazzling and decaying parts – white dogwood flowers in the garden of a church, radiant in the daylight, a homeless old man sleeping in the shade of the tree using his artificial leg for a pillow – so much here is extreme and outrageous. But we take pleasure in the wide streets and the ordered ranks and rows of the large city blocks; the composition of the city gives us a sense of the mighty will of the people who planned and built New York. Because we live in Tokyo, a chaotic place by contrast, we miss the simple act of just turning left or right for a few blocks after getting off a bus or exiting the subway, both of which seem to run almost all the time, and readily locating a destination along the long north-south axis of Manhattan.

It was May 1984 when we began taking photographs. From then until mid-September, we walked all over Manhattan and part of Brooklyn with our camera and tripod nearly every day. As a side benefit, we became very knowledgeable about antiques stores, flea markets, and coffee shops with bathrooms.

When a dozen rolls of our Kodachromes had been developed, Kohei Onishi encouraged us, saying, "This is going to be an exciting project." When the roll count reached twenty, Takehiko Kamei told us, "You have a good eye!" When the number of selected slides reached twelve hundred, Sol LeWitt said, "It's a good idea to take a lot of shots and to make a big catalog-kind of book." And when we reached two thousand, Takashi Nakahata shouted, "I'll get you a publisher!" The summer of the following year, we walked everywhere reshooting.

Suggestions and support also came from Domenick Capobianco, Alan Finkel, David Finkbeiner, Joseph Montague, Elfi Shuselka, Anna Wong, and Jo Watanabe.

Nobuyuki Endo of TOTO Publishing and Ryozo Sakurai of Crescent provided us with assistance in finishing this complex project. This book was completed thanks to the efforts of all these people. We thank them all very much.

BIBLIOGRAPHY

Black, Mary. *Old New York in Early Photographs: Eighteen Fifty-Three to Nineteen Hundred & One.* New York: Dover Publications, 1973.

Brolin, Brent C. *Flight of Fancy – The Banishment and Return of Ornament.* New York: St. Martin's Press, 1985.

Ellis, Edward R. *The Epic of New York City: A Narrative History.* New York: Marboro Books, 1990.

Gayle, Margot, and Edmund Gillon, Jr. *Cast-Iron Architecture in New York.* New York: Dover Publications, 1974.

Goldstone, Harmon H., and Martha Dalrymple. *History Preserved: A Guide to New York City Landmarks and Historic Districts.* New York: Simon & Schuster, 1974.

Halpern, John. *New York / New York, an Architectural Portfolio.* New York: Dutton, 1978.

Harris, Cyril M. *Illustrated Dictionary of Historic Architecture.* New York: Dover Publications, 1983.

Hersey, George. *The Lost Meaning of Classical Architecture: Speculations on Ornament from Vitruvius to Venturi.* Cambridge, MA and London: The MIT Press, 1988.

Huxtable, Ada Louise. *Classic New York.* New York: Dover Publications, 1964.

Jacoby, Stephen M. *Architectural Sculpture in New York.* Magnolia, MA: Peter Smith, 1975.

Kouwenhoven, John. *The Columbia Historical Portrait of New York.* New York: Doubleday, 1953. Reprint. New York: Icon Editions, Harper & Row, 1972.

Lewis, Philippa, and Gillian Darley. *Dictionary of Ornament.* New York: Pantheon Books, 1986.

Nuttgens, Patrick J. *The Pocket Guide to Architecture.* New York: Simon & Schuster, 1981.

Rider, Fremont. *Rider's New York City.* New York: Macmillan, 1924.

Rifkind, Carole. *Field Guide to American Architecture.* New York: New American Library/Dutton, 1980.

Silver, Nathan. *The Lost New York.* New York: Random House, 1991.

Still, Bayrd. *Mirror for Gotham: New York as Seen by Contemporaries from Dutch Days to the Present.* New York: Fordham University Press, 1994.

Stokes, Phelps N. *The Iconography of Manhatten Island.* Reprint. New York: Arno Press, 1967.

Tauranac, John. *Essential New York.* New York: Holt, Rinehart & Winston, 1979.

Tunick, Susan. *Field Guide to Apartment Building Architecture.* New York: Friends of Terra Cotta/N.Y.S., 1986.

Tunick, Susan. *SITES 18, Magazine "Architectural Terra Cotta."* New York: Lumen, 1986.

White, Norvel, and Elliot Willensky. *AIA Guide to New York City.* New York: Macmillan, 1978.